Nature's CELEBRATION

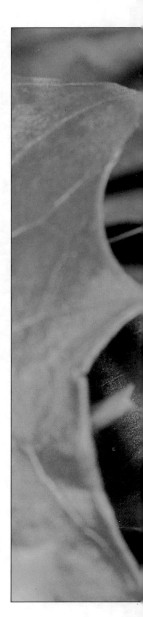

*L*awns not mown...
overgrown.

2

$\mathcal{B}$lack queen waits,
anticipates...

$\mathcal{B}$erries ripen.

Secrets open.

Tendrils curl,
flowers unfurl.

6

$\mathcal{C}$reatures crouch.

$\mathcal{D}$ewdrops drench.

Eggs are plundered,
meals attended.

$f$ugitive dares
scarcely breathe.

$f$orelegs wave.

Guests
arrive.

*T*ravelers rest.

*T*rapeze-lings nest.

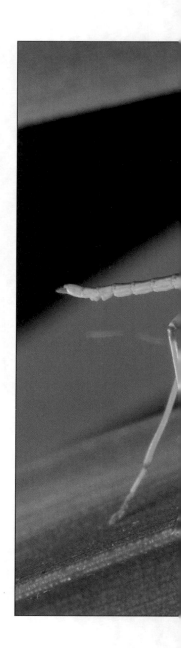

$\mathcal{B}$ent stick limbs
abandon skin.

$\mathcal{H}$unters net.

$\mathcal{P}$artners mate.

Sweetness flows.

Wings repose.

*N*eglected nature celebrates.